Gyerekkorunk csingteveseinek emlékére!

Sok szeretettel:

Szilvi

For my niece and nephew, Dorina and Mark.

Not the same

by Szilvia Veber

It was a beautiful day in Ocean Land.

Ollie and his little friends Dory, Wally and Foamy were playing hide and seek, when the weather all of a sudden turned stormy.

"Let's go into the corals. It will keep us safe. Hurry!!" said Dory. They all followed her in a line. First Wally, then Foamy and last Ollie.

But before Ollie reached the corals, a waterspout caught him and span him away.

Ollie shouted "Help! Help!". Foamy tried to catch him, but sadly, it was too late. Ollie was spinning around and around far far away from his neighbourhood. He was spinning so fast that he slipped out of his house losing everything.

When the waterspout finally spat him out, he found himself in an unknown place.

He looked around and did not see his friends. He called out for them. "Foaaamy! Doooryyyy! Can you hear me?" But there was no reply.

Ollie was very sad. He sat down next to a rock and started to cry.

"I miss my home… I miss my friends. I feel lonely here" he said.

"Why are you sobbing so sadly, little turtle?" asked Mr Krab.
"A tornado dropped me here and I don't know where here is.
I've lost my home with all my toys and all my friends" sniffed Ollie.

"That sounds very sad. Losing everything can be very upsetting and difficult. I'd like to help you , little turtle." said Mr. Krab.
"It's Ollie."

When they arrived at the school, Mrs Shelly invited Ollie to her special room, where she kept her toys.

I used to have loads of toys too but the waterspout took them. My favourite toy was Hopper Rabbit and he always slept with me." Ollie said sadly.

"Sounds like he was very important for you. It must be difficult not having him anymore" said Mrs Shelly.
"It is. You know, my home was very cosy and friendly... I miss my home so much. And my friends."
said Ollie with a tear in his eye.

"I know you do, and it is okay to miss them. I would miss them too, but you will make new friends and will find a new home here in Marina Land."
"Why can't I get my old house?" asked Ollie.
"Because the waterspout dropped it somewhere, we don't know where. And the ocean is too big to find such small things".

Ollie seemed sad but understood what Mrs Shelly said.
"I think, Ollie, you are a very brave little turtle and
I'd like to ask you to look after my Snuggabear.
I know he would love to be your new toy."

Weeks passed and Ollie started to like Marina Land. He had new friends from school and Mrs Shelly helped him to choose his new house. He still thought about Ocean Land, his friends and his toys but he knew that it would not be safe to go back to Ocean Land. Slowly Marina Land became his new home. A place, where he felt safe.

© 2022 Szilvia Veber. All rights reserved.

Printed in Great Britain
by Amazon

84032574R00020